Living in the Abyss

Living in the Abyss

Poems by

Katrina N. Jirik, Ph.D.

© 2023 Katrina N. Jirik, Ph.D. All rights reserved.
This material may not be reproduced in any form, published,
reprinted, recorded, performed, broadcast,
rewritten or redistributed without
the explicit permission of Katrina N. Jirik, Ph.D.
All such actions are strictly prohibited by law.

Cover design by Shay Culligan
DAuthor photo by Barbara Jirik
Cover image by Pawel Czerwinski via unsplash

ISBN: 978-1-63980-330-9

Kelsay Books
502 South 1040 East, A-119
American Fork, Utah 84003
Kelsaybooks.com

Acknowledgments

I want to thank my gifted therapist, Dave, and my mom, Barbara, who helped me climb out of the abyss and learn to live in a vastly different world.

Also, to my family, friends, colleagues, friends of friends, and all my good people, thank you for helping me stay in this wonderful world outside of the abyss.

Preface

Dear Readers,

I want to invite you into my poetry book. But first, I want to tell you some things to help you interact with it. *Living in the Abyss* is an attempt to describe what it is like to live with complex post-traumatic stress disorder (CPTSD). It could not have been written while I was living there. This doesn't mean that I no longer have CPTSD, but rather that, for the most part, it no longer controls my life.

One of the comments I hear a lot from people with CPTSD is that "I feel so alone; nobody understands what it is like!" I wrote this book to put into words the complicated and sometimes overwhelming internal life living with CPTSD can be. I hope that reading the book may resonate with you to help you realize you are not alone. And that, by giving it to friends, family, and, perhaps, even therapists, the book may help them understand what your inner life may be like.

This book is, in many ways, very dark, just as CPTSD is often very dark. It's meant to be read one poem at a time, not all at once. My reviewers who tried to read it all at once were overwhelmed, and I don't wish that for you, my readers. My wish is that, even in the darkness, you find some comfort in knowing you are not alone.

Katrina N. Jirik, Ph.D.

Contents

Incomprehensible Trauma Words	15
Noise	17
Nightmares	19
Twilight Time	21
Lost Little Girl	23
Lost	24
The Survivor	25
Darkness	26
Connections to Loneliness	27
Terror	30
Business Section	32
Monotony	33
Confusion	35
A Visit	37
Survival	39
Tornado	40
The Unexpected	41
Recycled Time	43
Anticipation	45
A Fetal Ball	47
When It Is More Than One	49
Positive Mismatch	51
Darkness to Dawn	53
Parasite	54
Specimen	56
Belonging	59
Dissociation	61
Losing Autonomy	62
Broken Promises	63
Fantasy and Reality	64
Is It Real?	66
Options	68
Ordinary Things	70

Trust	72
Trauma Shroud	74
The Plague	76
Detonations	77
You're Safe	78
The Void	79
Life, Unimaginable	80
Power	82
Razor Wire	83
Retribution	86
Resilience	89
Terror's Secret	92
The Return	94
Smog	96

Incomprehensible Trauma Words

Words flowing over your body,
Bringing no comprehension to the mind buried in trauma.
Because trauma does not allow meaning
That does not serve its destructive purpose
There is no place for ambiguity
For memory of a different time
By definition, the trauma only articulates
The chasm of fear, of terror
As it insidiously works to
Encapsulate you in its trauma shroud

Words echo in your brain
As you attempt to understand
The meaning originally intended
But words are an infinite confusion
Because trauma has corrupted them
Turning positives into a hellscape
Where meanings are imbued
With the colors of destruction
Flashing warning signs
Beware, danger, pain ahead.

The words are less than meaningless
For they all convey the same intent
No differentiation possible because
They offer no guidance in how to respond.
Other than rage or scream or hide
As you tremble against
The tripwire the trauma has installed in your brain
Not understanding the reactions
Of the people around you
As you struggle to explain

That trauma's language of words
Is so vastly different
That it is like a language all its own
A language you have been taught
In excruciating detail
But is impossible to describe
To those outside of trauma's powerful grasp
For they cannot contemplate
A vocabulary so deranged
Based on isolation and fear

And sometimes you wonder
If you are from a different planet
Or were birthed by monsters
Inhabiting secret caves
Who pushed you out
Into the confusing world
That others call reality
The words flow over your body.
As you attempt to interpret them,
Away from the trauma, usually without success.

Noise

When the street noise
Coalesces into an unholy roar
Of sirens and screams and gunfire
Of screeching brakes
Of breaking glass and crashing cars
And you are the only one who hears it
When everyone else only hears
Mortal silence
Then you know
That the terror
That haunts your nightmares
Has broken loose
And now lives in
Your waking hours

You now have no respite
No way to hide from the
Endless, persistent, ear-splitting sounds
That make you cover
Your ears, wishing for headphones
Wishing for anything
To dampen the sound
But knowing that if the street noise lessens
Its replacement will be much worse
The maniacal laughter
The whispered slurs
You're worthless
You're not even
A real human

And the wider world
Hears nothing
No street noise
No fetid whispers
It hears only the silence
Of oblivion
So, it offers no safe haven
No refuge from your terror
Because it cannot comprehend
What it chooses
Not to hear
And so it leaves you
Ostracized into that world of noise
Wondering if silence is the equivalent of death.

Nightmares

When night falls and the world goes quiet
You fall into a restless oblivion
Your internal vigilance on alert
For any sign of encroaching terror
In stealthy footsteps creeping across polished floors
Or coughs hastily covered to mute the sound
Or the opening of the bedroom door
That sends a small waft of air into the room
Bringing you instantly aware
Assuming terror, no matter the intent of the sound
Knowing that a quiet night of restful sleep
Is a fantasy
Because you are always on alert
Always vigilant, always in need of protecting yourself
Always in a state of preparedness
To be wide awake,
Almost as if you can anticipate
The coming avalanche of fearful specters
That creep into your nights from your withered days.

But for some reason, your vigilance doesn't extend to your dreams
It can't predict what frightening images
Will stalk you as you try to escape
There is no warning system inside you
That warns you when those nightmares are coming
Those dreams of being lost
Among crowds of people
No one responding to your pleas for help
Instead, pushing you back
Never letting you move forward
Only backward, into the clutching arms of terror
People who can't be bothered to see you
Who have their own worldview

In which your existence is no more important
Than a small fly, to be brushed off and ignored
And still you try to plunge forward
Until you wake up screaming
Knowing you should have tried harder to stay awake
Or at least in the oblivion where your vigilance operates

You're told you are a light sleeper
But that has nothing to do with your reality
You live in a world where the terror of your days
Dances through your nighttime hours
Never stopping, never offering even a brief respite
Where terror manipulates new abominations
Setting up new nightmare traps
Terrors you haven't experienced yet
Giving you warning that the worst is yet to come,
That even your wakeful imagination could not contemplate.
And your memories of those terror-stricken dreams
Wash over you as morning approaches
Arming your internal vigilance with awareness
Of unexplored terror possibilities
Of potential ticking time bombs
Waiting in some hidden corner of your day
Or stalking you with stealth
Waiting for the perfect time to implode your life
Until again you sleep in terror's nightmare realm.

Twilight Time

The sun rose on another hot day
The whine of the broken air-conditioner
Letting you know it was not going to cool anything.
The sweat outline of your body
Increasing your discomfort
Yet you dare not move
Or indicate that you're awake
Because if you're awake
You have to transition from your nightmares
To your omnipresent daytime horrors
And just for a few minutes
In that twilight state
Between asleep and awake
You have respite from
The atrocity that others have made your life.
And you linger there
Hoping that somewhere in that mystical time
Between dusk and dawn
A miracle occurred or even a small positive event
That releases you from the mind-numbing
Repetition of excruciating trauma.

In that brief twilight time
You manage a fluttering of something resembling hope
Knowing that when you finally open your eyes
It will vanish into a dreamscape
Of other impossibilities
And so you struggle to stay wrapped
In the realm of possibilities
Knowing that you will ultimately fail
But yearning so desperately for an alternative beginning
To another blighted day
Trying to conjure up one positive thing

That might happen in the coming day
Just one thing to cradle close
As you fall asleep
One thing to shield you
From the terrifying nightmares
That replay the trauma
Offering new twists
New transformations
That leave you broken, unprotected
But before you can search out
That one potential positive thing
Your eyes open and you are no longer
In that indistinct realm of possibility
Your day begins
And the hot sun beats down on you
Just one more negative to add to your soul-crushing day.

Lost Little Girl

Lost outside of the reaches of time and space,
Lost outside the reaches of human touch,
Lost outside the reaches of compassionate connection,
Lost little girl.

Lost within the echoing memories,
Lost within the roaring silence,
Lost within the failing turmoil,
Lost little girl.

Lost among the gathering ghosts,
Lost among the angels defiled,
Lost among the scattered spirits,
Lost little girl.

Lost little girl,
Is anyone searching?
Lost little girl,
Does anyone care?

Lost little girl,
Does anyone love you?
Lost little girl,
Is there anyone there?

Lost

Lost in the swirling eddies of confusion,
Immersed in turbulent undertows of memory,
Tossed as flotsam on abandoned shorelines
Of unknown feelings and perplexing options.

Clanging bells annul the internal silence.
Whining whistles invade the consciousness.
Screeching brakes precede the crash
Of conflicting memories and unexplored possibilities.

Lost among the crowds of realities,
Immersed in the babble uncomprehended,
Tossed over constructed barriers
Of previous panics and damaged emotions.

Screaming intensifies the immense loneliness.
Wailing intrudes upon rare contemplation.
Roaring hovers over the untold conceptions
Of possible potentials and lost little girls.

The Survivor

Returning to the site of intolerable devastation, the survivor
Excavates the memories, bringing intractable pain.
The empty ground where the destruction took place
Serves only to reinforce the emptiness of the emotional reservoir.

The world moves on and by.
But the survivor remains stationary,
Lost in the timeless connection with past,
Reliving the terror that comes with the territory.
Wondering whether the vindictiveness belongs to God or to man.

The crowds move on and by.
But the survivor remains solitary,
Clutched in the jaws of awful remembering,
Searching in vain for some pleasant connection.
Alone with the screaming, alone and afraid.

Darkness

The daytime sun provided little warmth
Even as its heat caused bodies to sweat.
The miasma of waste and water shimmered off the street in waves.
The warmth enclosed away from the body, leaving ice.

And the fan whirred in the silent house.
Red, blood red, liquid oozed down the stairs
Congealing, staining, impossible to clean.
Illuminated by the afternoon light,
Awaiting darkness to hide the perversity.

And yet, the horror existed, outside the bounds of righteousness.
Calmly, quietly, pretentiously, terrifyingly,
The salvation ever silenced by its powerful existence.
The life embalmed in the never attained rescue.

The ever-present screaming never coming forth
Seen only in the trembling, silent body.
Chilled, as if the horror had entombed the heat.
The body eviscerated into small pieces of humanity.

And the darkness did not signify safety.
It merely allowed the visibility of the terror to recede,
Allowed the contaminated soul to slumber.
The contagion brought by horror returning with the sun.

Connections to Loneliness

In the midst of crowds you stand alone
Encased in a shimmer of invisibility
That forces you to move through
The physical environment without recognition
By any of its inhabitants
Amid, yet apart
Never interacting on the same plane

For you are alone with the wellspring
Of ever-present fear
Of retribution, for what
You have no idea
Having learned that connections
Only bring uncertainty and trauma
Ending in the necessity of complete withdrawal

You listen to the voices
Not able to process the sounds
Because they are formed around concepts
That were tainted, poisoned
When your learning was maliciously corrupted
Before you even knew
That you lived isolated in a trauma life

Muted because there are no connections
No vocabulary, no interpersonal anything
That allows you to reach out
Hoping for some sort of recognition
Of your existence
Even if there is no understanding
That you live a trauma life

That shimmer of invisibility
Constrains your ability to reach out
Because as you try to evade the shimmer
It entwines your arm
Using fear to prevent your movement
Your desire for connections
Adding another layer of gossamer steel fabric

Until there seems to be no way out
And the crowd of people has no way
To recognize the shimmer
Holds you in captivity
Maintaining its potent stranglehold
While you struggle to
Protect at least a shred of your humanity

And the connections among people
Are impossible for you to understand
Because the shimmer distorts
The interactions, much like a shattered mirror
Provides no coherent image
So you glean only pieces
Of scattered reflections

You exist only within yourself
Isolated, confused, lonely
With limited understanding of the concepts
Because it is what always has been
You're ensnared in your present
Because there was no different past
To compare it to, no future to anticipate change

So you exist within the shimmer
Moving hesitantly in the incomprehensible world
Trying to reconstruct the mirror shards
Until you realize that you
No longer have all the pieces
That you are alone
Your only connection is to soul-draining aloneness.

Terror

Sometimes the terror is silent,
Lurking around the edges of your awareness
That's when it is the most dangerous
Hiding, but not perfectly concealed
Letting wisps of its frightening essence
Curl around you, demanding notice,
But keeping its malevolence disguised, for the moment
Searching, ever searching for your weaknesses
Looking for a way in, to marvel at its destructive power.
Its insidious, mocking presence,
Swirling around every part of your being
Never leaving, invading even your dreams
There is no rest, no peace, only constant vigilance
Dreading the outcome when the inevitable happens
And the terror finds its opening,
When you weren't able to beat it back
It roars into you, sounding like the keening of an F5 tornado
Screeching ever louder, the tone escalating up the scale
Combining with your screaming
Until the skies open to blazing lightning
And overwhelming thunder
And you tremble as the terror triumphantly encases you,
Screeching, crying, but to little effect,
The terror having no purpose other than destruction
No remorse, no compassion, only the desire to magnify its power
It searches for any sense of happiness or peace inside you
Then uses its razor-sharp teeth to rend them asunder
Seeming to relish its destructive force,
But always leaving a tidbit,
A small remembrance of its power to reap annihilation,
At a time of its choosing
And when it recedes, it never fully leaves
Going back to lurking, a reminder that you are never safe

That the terror will invade you at a time of its choosing
That your defenses, no matter how much you reinforce them
May delay the terror's inquisition
But can never successfully repel its attacks
Because the terror owns you
And will not relinquish you
Because you have become terror's trophy,
The symbol of its power of devastation.

Business Section

Left in a box on the side of the dirt road
Were the remnants of unheard crying.
The body wrapped in old newspapers
Soaked with the child's undried tears.
A tiny fist poking through
A rip in the business section,
Telling the people that business is booming,
Booming too loud to attend the child's crying,
Frozen in time in a box on the road.

Monotony

The days drag on
Melting into timeless drudgery
Flowing into one another
With no demarcation
Darkness to light to darkness, again
A monotony of everlasting sameness
An intimate knowledge
With the continuous trauma
And you sometimes wish
That the trauma would either
Escalate or de-escalate
Anything to indicate
It was a day with a difference
A difference you could etch
In your memory
Something that let you know
That you existed
Rather than just inhabited
An eternal miasma
Of the repetitive, soulless trauma

And people think it is all in your head
Which is in some sense true
But you didn't initiate
The experiences that put
The trauma in your head
You were taught,
So exquisitely taught
Through constant repetition
And no possible alternatives
That the trauma was the truth
Of your existence
Of your worth
Of your identity

You had no way
To comprehend the massive lie
The trauma told your brain
As it shouted at you during the day
And whispered in your dreams
Leaving you no escape

And the trauma life
You live is your reality
It isn't just in your head
It sweeps and swirls
Throughout your entire body
It orchestrates
A symphony of despair
A cacophony of endless fear
A song of endless, slow-moving eradication
Until there is almost
Nothing left inside of you
Your protective barricades
Dismembered faster than
You can reconstruct them
And your safe place
If you ever had one
Becomes smaller, infinitely smaller
Until it ultimately ceases to exist
Forcing you into the ongoing
Monotony of everlasting trauma

Confusion

When you build pillars of security
To anchor yourself against
The gale force winds of trauma
You situate yourself within a box
Reinforcing the beams
Adding Kevlar sheeting to the walls
Secreting yourself in aloneness
Protecting yourself against the fear
The trauma brings as it
Howls against your structure
Searching for a crevice to
Blow off the roof
And collapse those reinforced pillars
And you foolishly convince yourself that
You are safe, you are protected

But somehow you forgot
Or nobody told you
That trauma is a shapeshifter
Capable of transforming
Into a different manifestation of terror
Your thick walls are no defense
Against starvation of your body and soul
As the wind has whipped up
A flood that starts to slowly invade
Your security structure
As you desperately try
To find that secretive bolt hole
Trying to remember
If you even built one
Or if you now succumb to trauma's fury

And if you find that escape hatch
Where are you escaping to?
You've left your pillars of security
Awash in the flood
And you stand out in the open
Frozen
Trying to determine
If you should rage against the terror
Kicking, screaming, hitting
To let someone, anyone
Know you exist
Or try to make yourself invisible
Curled up and unresponsive
Hidden in plain view
A thing to be disposed

And how do you decide
In that catatonic state of despair
When safety is something
That is so nebulous
To you
That you cannot conceive
Any possible configuration
That mitigates the terror of trauma
That gives even a marginal direction
To a middle space
Between the activity of rage
And the nothingness of surrender
Where you live in a
A surrealistic environment
Without knowledge of who you are.

A Visit

In the early morning you wake
And know with certainty
That uninvited visitors have come
For an undetermined length of time
Sometimes a day, sometimes a month
Sometimes even longer
And they simply refuse your request to leave

You've known their names
For what seems like an eternity
Genghis Khan and Attila the Hun
Bent of destruction and mayhem
The Boys are clustered in your brain
Warring constantly to produce
Toxic, harmful outcomes

Outcomes that they generate
To push you into
A cauldron of fear, uncertainty, and despair
Destroying any attempts of help
From outside sources
Leaving you to slip back
Into the cauldron

As the Boys have slicken the sides
With messages of trauma
Of self-destruction
As the only acceptable outcome
After all, their mission is not salvation
They seek vengeance
Against your desire to exist

And the world does not see
That you are mired in a cauldron
With little hope of escape
They see you withdrawn into a shaking ball
Or a pale, unreactive statue
Or screaming and kicking to try to escape
But they don't know these are escape attempts

They just write you off as a person
Who needs to be confined,
Isolated, away from humanity
Not to protect you, but to protect them
And they don't understand the devastation
A visit from the Boys entails
And so you are immensely alone

Trying to survive, trying to push the Boys
Back into the past where they belong
Along with the trauma that created them
Trying to figure a way to empty the cauldron
Or reach out to the hand offering assistance
Knowing it will most likely end in failure
And you wonder if it is worth the effort.

Survival

Shards of sunlight lay shattered around her,
Sharp edges of shadows are etched on the wall.
Sorrow and silence invade her memories,
Spasms of rage storm mostly internal.
Sparks of survival resist being smothered
Somewhere in stillness the soul craves redeeming
Silently struggling to maintain her life.

Tornado

When you are sitting in the eye of the tornado
You are safe and at peace,
But you are not part of the real world.
To enter that world, you have to cross the violent, spiraling bands
Of chaotic, ferocious destruction.
The likelihood of safely traveling from the eye to the world is
Fraught with terror, fear, and devastating horror,
And success is so often hopeless.
The scars so horrendous that survival is precarious
As your life is strewn about in the winds of abomination.
The choice to leave that eye means accepting
An almost insurmountable mountain of risk.
It's not an easily made choice
To struggle with the winds of overwhelming destruction
Requires a recognition of a possible life that
Is worthy of the exhaustive fight,
That is worth failing innumerable times,
Each time leaving new scars, new terrors, new fears,
Trying to find a different plan to escape,
Knowing that you may ultimately give up
Because the winds are too strong,
That there are no more pieces of you left
To bear destruction brought on by the wind.
So you either stay inside the eye
In solitary confinement, locked inside yourself
Or fling the last small bits of yourself into the wind
In hope of spinning out on the other side
Or meeting death as destruction destroys
Your last remaining remnant.

The Unexpected

In the brightness of the day, the darkness roars in
Not as storm clouds blocking the sun
Not as a drawn window shade to cut down glare
No, the darkness comes
Because terror slipped its bonds of containment
And enveloped your body with its unholy contamination.

What was it this time that let the terror in?

Was it the sound of somebody saying, hey,
That to most people signals a friend approaching,
But what you hear is the precursor to being hit
A premonition of pain, of helplessness
Terror being unable to distinguish a benign occurrence.

Was it the smell of cigarettes?
Your brain can't limit itself to thinking it's a bad habit.
It immediately flashes to what it meant in the past,
Ignored for hours, not knowing if you would get fed,
Not knowing if she would even remember you existed.

Was it the sudden movement
You caught out of the corner of your eye?
A movement with no inherent meaning to anyone else
But to you it is the antecedent of something bad approaching,
A warning to take cover, to protect your body
To run and hide or curl up into a ball.

Was it the woman dressed in white
With her hair pulled back away from her face,
A stranger, but much of your abuse was committed by people,
Whose names you didn't know.
And you need to decide if you turn away or walk past,
Though often these choices don't appear in your brain
And you stand rooted in place, a statue.

Was it the unexpected touch on your shoulder?
Offered by a friend, but perceived as a threat
Because you weren't prepared,
You didn't have time to tell your brain it was OK.
You shudder, pull away, and search for a benign explanation
But behind your false front,
Your heart races because the door to terror has been opened.

The terror lies in wait for the unexpected.
It has taught you well, that no place is safe,
It has fine-tuned your brain
To exquisite awareness that it is ever-present,
That there is nothing in your world that it hasn't corrupted
Because it owns you.

Recycled Time

Quietly, time stops, not for an instant, not for an hour, not for a day
It stops, even as the day moves into night and back again to dawn.
It's your internal clock that stops, while everyone else's moves on
It stops because you have lost your ability to process time
Time, meaning moving forward into the future,
A future you cannot even begin to contemplate
As your fear reverberates, spinning in concentric circles,
Never allowing even the potential of breaking free.

Time only moves backward, then replays the trauma
On an infinite loop, over and over and over again
Never varying, even as you hope for just a slight variation
A variation that lets you know you are alive
But time just continues to cycle,
You're lost within the pain and fear
It's all-encompassing, leaving no place,
No hope, no embodiment of humanity
Your internal clock at odds with humanity's sense
Of forward-moving time
At odds with possibilities not enthroned in fear.

You are encased in the shroud of unmoving time
Situated in a cauldron of caustic fear
Slowly being eaten away, erased by fear's acidic miasma
The toxic vapors invading your lungs
Until you die a thousand deaths
As your time clock recycles the fear again,
Ever more tangible, insidious, reeking of death
Escape never possible,
Only endless currents of fear constricting you

Your time has stopped,
But you cannot even have the release of death
For your trauma is ongoing, living in your body,
Your brain finding no alternative, no placebo, no comfort
Escape impossible to orchestrate
Because you have no forward-moving time
You have no assistance, only callous misunderstanding
From people who live with time moving onward
While you ricochet in the destructiveness of unchanging time.

Anticipation

It's noon and the day is half over
And you haven't felt the onslaught of fear, yet.
But while others might rejoice that
It hasn't made an appearance
Thinking that it's been vanquished
Defeated, left behind, conquered
You know differently
You know it is simply waiting
Gaining strength, plotting destruction
Seething beneath its façade of peaceful iniquity
And the hair on the back of your neck
Stands upright, like radar scanning the horizon
Looking for warning signs, glimmers of hostility
Hoping to offer a few seconds to prepare
Your defenses, although it's usually insufficient
For protecting you.
Your brain conjuring possible escapes
Rapidly discarding the hundreds of failed attempts
And you become more agitated
More anxiety-ridden, more fearful
Totally at odds with the peaceful vista
Spread out around you
Deep breathing doing nothing to calm
Your racing heart
Your hands clenching
As you scan that vista for a hiding place
A sanctuary, a safe place
That is still a secret you hold inside
Somewhere the fear hasn't contaminated, yet
Knowing that it is unlikely to exist
Because the fear lives inside of you
Growing ever more powerful
Ever more destructive

To your ability to live in the peaceful vista
Because you have no conception of how to contain it
No strategy to confine it to the past.
It lives in you as a malevolent parasite
Tearing through your defenses
Taking you to the brink of death
Of annihilation
But preserving just enough of you
To feed off of, to magnify its power.
And you stare out into nothingness
Waiting for the inevitable devastation
The anticipation almost worse
Than the actual forthcoming calamity
Wondering if you have ten minutes, or an hour
Each second seeming like an eternity
Sapping your energy
Your ability to interact
Because the unholy terror
Commands you,
Entirely.

A Fetal Ball

In the dark corner of your closet
You curl up into a fetal ball
With your head tucked to your chest
And your arms and legs
Pulled up tight to protect your belly
You're buried under a pile of dirty laundry
Trying to hold your breath
But your heart beats so fast and so loud
That you know you cannot escape.
The persistent terror will hear
It's frantic beating
And will slowly burrow under your safety pile
Giving you the faint hope
That you can contain it
That your defenses are strong enough
To ward it off, this time
But then it pounces
Fast, too fast to guard against
Using your shallow breathing
As a gateway into your body
Into the fragile construction of your soul
And you have no defenses
Against its complete immobilization of your body
Your screams never making it
Out of your lungs
Constricted by the force of the terror
And you cannot move from your fetal ball
Because that opens up your body
To terror's punishment
The futile shaking that rattles your bones
And the rigid clamp of your teeth
Threatening to send you to a place
Where terror controls every aspect of you.

Pleading with disjointed thoughts
To have the terror recede
Just enough to catch a breath
To burrow deeper inside yourself
Hoping that somewhere a faint glimmer
Of who you are, will survive
Terror's onslaught
Knowing that you are totally alone
Left to your meager defenses
With no hope of rescue
Knowing that even if someone finds you
Curled in your fetal ball
Under the unwashed laundry
They won't understand your overwhelming need
To hide, to protect yourself
From the terror's relentless attacks
Because they lack any comprehension
Of its murderous, destructive invasions
That take over your entire self
Explanations stalled in a limbo
Because they have no sense of the enormity
That cannot be conveyed in words
Leaving you stranded on terror's island
Estranged from the world
From even your own sense of self
Intimately tied to the grotesqueness
Of unrelenting, malicious terror
A malignant curse upon your existence
As you try to curl up
Into an ever-smaller fetal ball.

When It Is More Than One

When you look into the eddies whirling through your head,
Can you put a name to each one?
Can you separate them into their component parts?
Fear, Terror, Loneliness, Horror, Abasement, Worthlessness,
Abandonment, Loss, Bereavement, Conflict, Confusion,
Anger, Conflagration, Defeated, Defective, Unlovable,
Furious, Hateful, Unwanted, Unhappy, Harmed, Hopeless,
Useless, Silenced, Petrified, Rejected, Depleted
Depersonalized, Devalued, Grotesque, Nobody,
Devastated, Annihilated, Invisible, and Helpless.

But you can't, can you, because they intertwine,
Masking some, while highlighting others.
It's complex, it's frustrating, it's unnerving.
It encompasses your whole being.
There is no place to start unraveling the trauma,
Because it is a tornado,
Strewing parts of you across the landscape of your life.
And you can't just get over it,
Because it's like trying to rebuild a barn
From the pieces the tornado has scattered over a forty-mile radius.

You can't go back to the beginning and start over
Because where is the beginning, where do you start
Unwinding the colossal empire trauma has built in your head.
The trauma will fight you if you try to dismantle it.
It resides in every hidden bit of you.
If you tug on the thread of Furious
It shines its light on Abandonment
And ties it to Defeated and Silenced
And the thread of Furious gets more tightly woven
Into your trauma shroud.
It's not just one thing and then another to deal with separately.
It's the huge conglomeration, melted one into another.

And the suggestion to relive your trauma in order to gain relief
Assumes it was a single event
With a beginning, a middle, and an end.
But you have no trauma timeline, no single event.
You live in a traumatic environment,
An ongoing source of degradation,
Of whirling eddies combining and separating
With no discernible reason.
And the new combinations bring new landmines
Primed for explosion,
With no ability to disarm them
As the eddies sweep you closer to destruction.
Your world a nightmare
Of confounding eddies of more than one thing.

Positive Mismatch

Almost protected against the overwhelming emotions
Happy, sad, joyful, angry, comfortable, worried.
What people don't understand
Is for you, there is no distinction
Nothing to differentiate one from another
They all belong to the same category: DANGEROUS
They give you no information about how to react
Because they are all encoded with fear
They shout, Get Away, Hide, Curl Up Inside Your Head
So you shrink away from feelings
Because nobody understands why happy things terrify you
And there is no way to explain that you don't comprehend happy
That happy is just another precursor to bad things happening
That sad just means the bad thing has happened
There is nothing to differentiate them other than time
How do you feel?
Has no answer other than, afraid
Because that is the only way
You know how to exist
Locked away where fear inhabits
Your entire world
Where positive feelings are only warning signs
Of negative outcomes, of terror, of pain,
Of being rejected by a world you don't understand
Love, trust, forgiveness, friendship
None of them have any meaning other than danger
And so they send you into cataclysms of protective arousal
Because the only thing you know is that you need protection
But people don't understand that
For you love and happy are threats
Threats to be met by pulling away
Retreating into the safe space you created in your head
Walled away from the threat that kindness represents

Your world unimaginable to the people around you
Who perceive no threat from positive things
And you have no way of making them understand
That what you need, so desperately desire
Is safety, is protection from the looming bad things
Because you have no way to describe
What safety is for you
It's a concept unanchored from reality for you
You know that you need it
But you have no words for something
You have no experience with
So you armor your protective shield
Against the impending danger
Lost in that world, alone and afraid.

Darkness to Dawn

Slowly the sun slides beneath the horizon
The gathering dusk fades into darkness
And a myriad of stars begins to dot the sky
For most of the world
This signals that rest and dreams are approaching
The soft comfort of cozy covers
Keeping you safe
Until you awaken to a new day

But for you, the coming darkness
Is a new beginning to your ongoing nightmare
You count the stars
By listing the traumas of the day
And give up when you reach fifty
Because the traumas are like a fifth column
Infiltrating behind your defenses
Waiting to attack you in your dreams

Darkness means you need
To heighten your vigilance
Sleeping lightly to ensure the terror
Can't slip in on stealthy butterfly wings
Because you don't want to awaken with pummeling fists
And eerie screams that are
Swallowed by the vast expanse of darkness
Leaving you in terror's void

And sleep never means peaceful rest
Your mind scrambling to erect defenses
To hide you away
From the vulnerability that comes with deep sleep
To keep you whole against the ravages of dark terror
To insulate you from the twinkling stars
Emitting rabid streams of turmoil and fear
And slowly the darkness fades to dawn.

Parasite

Creeping slowly into consciousness
As you pass the time with the breaking dawn
Wondering whether the nightmares were a reflection of past reality
Or a premonition of the terrors to be faced in the approaching day.
And you contemplate your defenses
Hoping they are strong enough to protect you
But realizing that hope is rather baseless
Because the terrors are a vast complex of interwoven traumas
With explosive devices indiscriminately planted
Throughout the tortures of your day
And even the bombs
That you intentionally avoided setting off yesterday
Have spun out to new, unknown locations
Waiting patiently for you to inadvertently set them off
And you know that even if you avoid their explosions today
They will await you tomorrow
And the day after and the day after that
Even the ones that exploded in your face
That tortured and humiliated you
And left you screaming into the void of retribution.
You know that the terror will rearm them
Taking your screams to build them back
Stronger, more horrifying, more deadly
And scattering them in places
You perceived to be safe
Waiting for you to unexpectedly hit the tripwire
And blowing you to bits
But not enough to kill you
For your death defeats the terror's purpose
It needs you alive, enmeshed in its bitter destruction
For without you to relive the terror
It vanishes into the ether, into nothingness
So it exerts all its power to break your spirit

To inhabit your soul
To feed off your screaming and horror
The infinite parasite, slowly destroying you
While keeping you ever under its domination
Never loosening its hold over you
And thus, you begin your day,
Wondering if survival is really worth the effort.

Specimen

The trauma fog drifts in slowly,
Like gentle wisps curling around the trees
And slowly, ever so slowly
The outline of the branches blur
Until they fade away
In the thickening fog.

And soon you can't see anything around you
You're encapsulated in the miasma of ongoing fear
Cut off from any connection,
Isolated from the visible world
No sound breaks through the shroud
Encasing you in unending silence

The trauma fog chills your body
Freezes you in a perpetual state
That takes away your senses
Leaving you in mothballs and cotton
Open for inspection
Like a specimen pinned to a board

Where you once had life
Now you are only a carcass
Examined under a professional's magnifying glass
Who doesn't ask how you came to be
The carcass instead of a living organism
Whose last breath was stolen.

And yet, you are not dead
Deep inside the pinned creature
There still exists that tiny spark of humanness
Buried deep, almost destroyed by the pinning process
But with no way out
Because the professional can't lose his specimen.

And you wonder why no one asks
About the constricting trauma fog
That wraps itself around you
Maybe, it's what no one wants to acknowledge
Because it eludes their skills of remediation
Easier instead to examine the mostly dead carcass.

And you are left screaming
Trying to escape, but
No one can hear you
Because who listens to a pinned-up carcass
A perceived dead specimen
A shadow, an enigma of the living organism.

And they wonder why
They can find no answers to the fog-like encasement
By examining the helpless specimen
The insidious process hidden from their opaque eyes
Because they don't understand
That they need the living organism

They don't understand the trauma fog
That slowly creeps into your soul
Disengaging you from the world of senses
Terrorizing your sense of connectedness
Obliterating your ability to reach out for comfort
Burying you until you are only a specimen.

And you wonder how you came
To belong to the category of specimen
How no one recognized your thickening shroud.
Could you maybe have done something different to alert them
To let them know you were still alive
That it wasn't your fault

And so you scream and try to unpin yourself
From the specimen board
But the fan noise covers up your screams
And the dislodged pin gets blamed on the junior colleague
Who reinserts it more firmly
Tethering you to the death-dealing specimen board

And you wonder why
You know the answers and
The ones who are trained to know, don't,
That you can hear the other specimens screaming
And the trained professionals are oblivious
To the cacophony of sound-seeking release

You wonder why they didn't notice the trauma fog
And stop it before it enveloped you
Why did they wait so long
That the only living part of you
Was almost indistinguishable
From a carcass?

Why did they think they could understand
The trauma fog
When they never went looking for it
While it was actively
Invading your body and soul
When it was holding you captive

Why didn't they listen to you
When you tried to tell about the trauma fog
Why did they only interact with specimens
Instead of the living organism
Why didn't they help you
Banish the trauma fog before it made you a specimen?

Belonging

It's lonely when you find yourself in the midst
Of three million people
And you have no relationship to any of them.
You're a child, shouldn't you have a connection
To at least one other person?
Where are the people you belong to?
Did you lose them somewhere?

Oh, now you remember
They lost you, because you weren't who they wanted.
You were worthless in their eyes,
A burden to be gotten rid of,
And so they did, letting you be someone else's responsibility.

But nobody ever really took responsibility.
Nobody ever let you belong to them.
You just existed as a money-making enterprise
To be ignored or moved to a different place.
The location changed, but nothing else, you still didn't belong.

And you met different people but never knew
What belonging felt like,
Because you were always told you were a burden
That you were worthless
And nobody wanted you to belong to them.

And you wonder what you did that was so awful
That out of three million people, there wasn't at least one person
To call your own, to belong to you.
It must have been something terrible
That dropped you into the realm of unwanted child.

You watched others get presents
But there were never any for you.
You heard stories being read
But so far away from you, the words were only murmurs
Because none of those connections were for you,
You were unworthy.

And after years of living with abandonment,
Even when surrounded by people
You're told you need to trust people.
Your problem, they say, is you think people are untrustworthy,
That you can never belong if you don't trust people to care for you,
That the past was what you created, you were responsible for it.

Yet you were a child, a child who belonged to no one,
Who lived with abandonment,
With constant messages of worthlessness,
Who never had a person to rely on because you were a burden,
Who didn't have the power to change anyone's perception,
That the only person worthy of your trust was yourself.

You discovered that attempting to trust other people
Resulted in failure, and came at a cost
Because every time you offered up a bit of trust
You offered up a bit of yourself
And when they threw away your trust,
They threw away a piece of you.

You were still a worthless burden
But you had no more pieces of yourself
To lose in the trashcan of people's refusal to care
So you learned to live in the isolated loneliness
Belonging only to yourself.

Dissociation

It seemed like such a small thing to the people
Who didn't even know they brought the terror into your life.
They didn't ask your opinion,
They simply took control of your body,
Manhandling it into contortions of perceived normality,
Their pernicious conceptions corrupting your world.

In the beginning, you were whole, unified, body and spirit,
In Genesis, the construction of safety, tied to your origin.
That unity threatened
Because you no longer controlled the outcome of your body.
Yet they were not satisfied with just your body,
They wanted your spirit, your soul,
For without your totality, they cannot destroy you.

So Genesis becomes the sanctuary for your spirit,
You cannot control the desecration of your body, but
You can attempt to keep your spirit safe,
You can hide yourself away from the terror, maybe,
Because they claw at your glass shield, seeking retribution
For your refusal to be totally destroyed.

If you're very lucky, your shield to Genesis will hold,
You'll be safe, but also aware of their destructiveness,
But as time goes by, the destructiveness creates cracks
And you build layers of safety until the outside world disappears.
You cease to monitor the world of your body
Enclosed in a realm of your spirit, effectively torn in two.

While they haven't reached your spirit,
You have buried it so deep in the safety of Genesis,
That unity becomes impossible,
You're fragmented beyond the hope of reconciliation,
Safety being the only consideration,
A safety that mimics death.

Losing Autonomy

In the sterile box, regimented, orderly, impersonal,
People flowing in and out of my box segment.
My body is there but my soul wanders in and out.
Questions rumble around but my ears
Proceed to process only bits of jargon.
Oblivion comes as my soul recedes,
Not quite making it back to my body.

Broken Promises

Echoes of broken promises
Slam against the kitchen door
Reverberate out across the backyard
Shattering over the fence
Swirling on the wind
Returning like doppler effect sirens
Louder, louder, close-together waves
Of blaring sound.
Suddenly fading into echoes,
The silence of broken promises screams.

Fantasy and Reality

Somewhere springtime comes with tulips and daffodils
Reds, yellows, pinks, and purples.
Gentle rains that nourish the lilacs
Bright blue skies and cotton ball, soft, white clouds
Entreat you to come outside after the long winter
Or at least that is what I imagine
As I stare at my pea soup green walls.

I tell myself there must be other colors of green
I see the variety in the TV shows
But maybe it's just a fantasy, like the animals that talk
Or grown-ups that seem to love their children.
Because the reality of my colors
Are pea soup green, dried blood brown, and death mask gray.

Somewhere music cuddles the soul
Violins, oboes, trumpets, and snare drums
And maybe an electric guitar or a piano
With a voice that sings its way into your soul,
Telling you that you are not alone.
At least that is my dream
As I listen to brash voices screaming at each other.
I tell myself that music must exist
Because the TV blares a bastardized version
Of what probably was once considered music
But maybe that is just my hope, another flight of fancy
A passionate concoction I put in place
To drown out the reality of the unending, toxic noise.

Somewhere there is caring, I'd like to believe that
Someone who comforts you when you're sad
Who joins you in make-believe castles and pirate ships
Who holds you close
And tells you stories where you are the shining star
Who holds your hand when you're afraid
At least that is what my dream of being cared for
Suggests might happen.

I tell myself that caring should exist
But even I know the fantasy I see on TV isn't real.
That the TV happy families are just a myth, a mirage
Because reality is being alone,
Isolated, cut off from human connections
And happy is something you don't understand
Having no experience with it,
It becomes just another out of reach fantasy.

I want to believe that somewhere these things exist
These frivolous, life-affirming things
But TV seems to be the only place I catch a glimpse of them
And TV is not real, it's a dreamlike fantasy
It's a pleasant piece of make-believe you can get lost in
In an attempt to escape from your actual reality.

My world, my real world,
Is a grotesque abomination of the fantasy TV depicts
It's drab and noisy and alienating,
A never-ending, all-encompassing death trap
A place of pitiful, marginalized existence
Where you have as much power as the pea soup green walls
A nonexistence, until in death you depart.

Is It Real?

The trembling recedes as the day drifts into night,
The darkness slowly covering the blood-red sky.
Softly the stars twinkle, keeping the light as mere flickers.
And the owl hoots somewhere beyond the rotting shed.
The soft summer breeze brings the booms of fireworks,
At least that is what your brain conjures up

As you lay in your bed, cowering in fear,
Wondering if this is the night that you will be abandoned
Or if this is the night when your nightmares become reality.
Or do they meld into one ghastly horror
Where you are left in the middle of a cornfield
With no way out.
You hear the sound of traffic
But no one stops to save you
Because your screams are muted
By the road noise that drifts over you.
Until finally, you have no screams left.

And you wonder if you are dreaming
Or have you created an analogy to describe your waking hours,
Wondering if this is the way you die
Abandoned and no longer capable of screaming,
No one around who responds to your pain,
No plan for survival coming to mind.

Or is it a reality that your brain tries to refashion
Into something less horrifying, less terrifying,
Because the reality is too monstrous to contemplate,
Too full of destructive forces that only know how to attack.
You've withstood those attacks over and over again.
They have sapped your strength to rebuff them.
Your brain attempting a protective cocoon,
But even its attempts cannot mitigate the unthinkable inhumanity,
It can only soften the edges
Telling you it's an owl hooting and stars twinkling,
But you know it is a lie, it's a living hell come to call.

Options

There is a sameness going on for days, for months.
The routine never changing,
Never allowing a simple particle of joy,
Even a small alteration, signifying human interaction, is forbidden,
Because you are not deemed worthy of life as a child.
You are an obligation, a task to be completed,
Before the caretaker can move on,
Taking care away from the next hunk
Of barely worthwhile humanity.

You're fed, most of the time.
You're clothed, usually.
You're sworn at, often.
You're washed, sometimes.
You're talked to, never.
You're left abandoned, always.
You're existing, barely.

Three choices await your deliberation
Capitulation or suicide or retrenchment

Capitulation to your life being worthless
Means you cease to exist as a separate entity.
You no longer have claim to childhood.
You are nothing more than a piece of protoplasm,
Mimicking the features of a human being.
A thing, to which things are done,
Because you gave up your right to object.

Suicide seems a bit extreme, especially since it's permanent,
But at least you retain some control,
Some sense that you cannot accept the loss of your individuality,
That capitulation is an unacceptable voyage into a virtual tomb,
That permanent escape is the preferable alternative,
To a lifeless existence in that hell of non-being.
Besides, there will be no one to grieve your death.

Retrenchment becomes an alternative
Because suicide is hard to accomplish as a child.
Retreating to a place inside you,
Where the lack of real human interaction doesn't matter,
Because you create your own world,
A world as unreal as the one outside of you,
But at least, you exist,
With almighty power to craft your protective world.

It's a world with variations, colors, music,
A place where playing is a natural right of childhood,
Where people exist like the families on TV,
Where celebrations are encouraged,
Where care is given, not taken.
And you tell me it's not real, just a figment of my imagination,
But given the choices,
I'll stay with my retrenchment, my happy place.

Ordinary Things

It was the ordinary things that slipped my notice,
The soft smiles, the gentle touch,
The favorite breakfast, the afternoon snack,
The bright pink tutu, the superhero cape,
The sled rushing down the hill,
The regal yellow tulips shining in the morning sun,
The curling up with my Grandma's afghan and a storybook,
The picnic in the backyard,
The fresh raspberries that jumped off the cane and into my mouth,
The birthday cake made just for me,
The joy of splashing in the puddles under a rainbow,
The spontaneous hug just because,
The love that wrapped around me because I was me.

These things slipped my notice
Because none of them belonged to me.
I had grim faces, utilitarian touch.
I had grape jelly sandwiches mixed with smushed green peas.
I had third-hand clothes, nothing that was just mine.
I was not allowed outside in winter, so I never knew about a sled.
I never saw a flower,
Only worn-away holes where grass used to be.
I never had a Grandma or a storybook.
I never had a picnic, it disrupted the routine.
Fresh fruit was not allowed, being too much of a hassle.
Nobody ever told me that I had a birthday,
So there was nothing to celebrate.
Joy was not allowed, puddles being only a nuisance.
No one believed in hugs, they were an unnecessary aberration.
Love was nowhere, non-existent,
And definitely not to be wasted on me.

All these ordinary things that people take for granted
Never existed in my world.
The implicit understanding of how the world was,
Was never mine, was unknowable,
As unattainable as touching a star.
Yet there exists the expectation
That I know these ordinary, wondrous things,
That we speak the same language of memory
That our experiences mirror each other's

Without the realization that my mirror was shattered eons ago.
I have no magic potion to reconstruct your mental juxtapositions
As your brain cannot conceive
Of a world devoid of ordinary things.
So we pass as strangers, a great ravine between us
For you believe with no reservations
That it is my job to understand ordinary things.
But I have no words for things I do not know.

Trust

You would think it would be simple to learn
To trust people who care for you
To trust people who are your friends
To trust your relatives to enjoy time with you
To trust yourself to be who you were meant to be
To trust your parents because you belong to them
To trust your ever-expanding world because they've guided you.

But what if there are no people that care for you?
What if nobody stays with you
When you are three and in the hospital?
What if there are no consistent people in your life
As you move from place to place?
What if no one listens, no one explains?
What if you are told you are worthless, a burden,
Who maybe only God could love?
What if you belonged to nobody?

So trust is not so simple
It requires that you give part of yourself to another person
"I trust you," opens you to despair when they don't carry through
Because you gave them part of yourself to care for
And they threw it away, perhaps unintentionally,
But that doesn't matter, you've still lost a piece of yourself.
And you learn to be more careful
As you only have so many pieces to lose.

So trust becomes more difficult because you have no experience
With people caring for you, people loving you
People being there when you are scared.
Do you rely on the derogatory labels pronounced upon you?
When trusting is an issue, can you believe the hurtful labels?
But there seem to be no alternatives,
At least none that you've heard
And there is no one to ask because you belong to no one.

You have no guidance, it's all up to you
To figure out who you are, who you were meant to be
And you are likely to mess it all up,
Relying on your child's understanding
Of the frightening world you live in
Hardly able to reason out options
Trust is not such a simple thing,
Its lack, a major deficit to being who you were meant to be.

Trauma Shroud

There is no safety when you live in a trauma shroud
Because when you live in safety
People have your back
They protect you
They help you carry the worry
They care for you
You get to be who you really are
You get to keep the things that are important to you
You get to laugh and sing and love
You get to exist in the world

But when you live in a trauma shroud
Everything revolves around terror
You are only partially alive
And you are never safe
Because terror infests every aspect of you
The terror shroud didn't just appear out of innocence
It was created by people
Who were careful weavers of swatches of terror
Weaving the swatches into your shroud
Leaving no possible means of escape

And the shroud contains no color
And permits no sound to penetrate
Enclosing you in unending terror
While invisible to the people around you
And they wonder why you react with fear
Not understanding that everything
Is filtered through your trauma shroud
Tainting everything, dyeing it in trauma motifs
Structuring your world with the aftereffects of terror
And the rubble of the perversity of your destruction

Your trauma shroud is the antithesis of safety
It permits no conception of safety to form
Negating any conception other than terror.
Confining you to living in nightmares
To embalming yourself in eternal vigilance
As your trauma shroud thickens
Wrapping you in the devastation of unending terror
Destroying even the idea of safety
Because your trauma shroud protects the terror, not you
So you forego the possibility of ever being you.

Because safety is incompatible with living in a trauma shroud.

The Plague

The Black Death of terror rampages through my brain,
The carrier rat indiscriminately infects my memories
Creating anguished, tortured death.
And the few surviving memories
Howl in grief at the irreparable destruction.

Detonations

Hidden in the recesses of questions
Lie the buried land mines,
Waiting for the unsuspecting query
To pull the trip wires,
Beginning the detonation
Of a series of explosions.
Each one louder, less controlled
Building until the cacophony
Overwhelms the consciousness,
Destroying the systems,
Creating desolation and emptiness,
Invading the soul,
Choking the source
Of dreams and commitments.
The noise permeates the interiors,
Cutting off connections,
Reducing life to screams
Of unending terror and intense pain,
Obstructing vision,
Turning the body to catatonic stone.
Screeches igniting
The implosion of self.
Rubble and wasteland
Are all that survive,
Destiny altered,
Rebuilding denied.
The flood tides of sound
Refused to be dammed,
Rampaging over the banks,
Demolishing the town,
Carrying away the interior contentments
Drowning the eternal juxtaposition
Of peaceful perceptions and knowledge unknown.

You're Safe

In the eerie aloneness of the empty 2 AM alley,
You skitter along, twisting your head from side to side,
And every tenth step, turning completely around,
Pretending you're safe and in control.

It's when those alleys appear during your board meeting,
Dancing under the grassy knoll that mimics your grave,
That you sit, a knot of writhing snakes in your belly,
Pretending you're safe and in control.

It's the silence of the mime's scream that echoes in your head.
The continuous shattering of crystal champagne glasses
That yowls you to sleep while you are
Pretending you're safe and in control.

The Void

Moving through the gathering gloom,
The sound is absorbed into silence.
The colors in the images fade
Washed out into oblivion.

The void consumes the senses,
Negating connections to reality,
Creating nothingness,
Emptiness expanding.

Shattering the carefully constructed universe,
Exploding the internal permutations,
Depleting the resources of emotion,
Chilling the flow of longing.

And the void expands
Into all available space,
Eroding the spirit
Betraying the soul.

Life, Unimaginable

In the early morning stillness
As you awaken to start the day
And dread fills your body
Seeping through every pore,
Your breathing shallow
Your heart beating like hummingbird wings
Your hands fisted and clammy
Your stomach clenched into a tight ball
You realize you have no other option
Than to get out of bed
Because at least if you're up
You have the remote possibility
Of outrunning the waking nightmare
That haunts your very soul

It's a faint possibility
More like a dream
Than a real option
But staying in bed
Means hopeless capitulation
To the demons in your head
So you arise
Beating back the hellscape
For the few minutes it takes to dress
But your toast tastes like sawdust
And you give up eating
Because the food can't move
Through the lump of fear
Twisting in your belly.

And you wonder if other people
Go through the same contortions
To start their day
And you wonder if not,
How it can be
So different, when
You both inhabit the same world
But maybe that's the issue
Your worlds are only superficially
The same, because
Who else calculates
How much terror resides
In each action you take
And how strong your defenses are.

And thus, you mask your pain
Shutting out as much of the world as possible
Because you have no energy
No strength, no understanding
To untie the Gordian knot
Of personal relationships
Intertwined with terrors
That attack your very existence
As you try to protect
That inner child from the trauma
Heaped upon you
Causing you to question
If your very existence
Is worth the effort to continue?

Power

The choices are poison, noose, or electrocution,
Suffocation, twisting body, or rigid shakings.
The caricature of evil,
Unrepentant,
Forcing elimination.

Envisioned,
As you crouch deep inside your body
Savagely protecting the minute core
Against the ongoing holocaust
Of degradation.

And you die slowly,
As the evil slices through you
Piece by piece
Tossing those intimate pieces of you
Into life's gutter.

And still you cling
To video dreams of murder.
Forgiveness being an unacceptable option
For resolving
Such personal destruction.

Razor Wire

Attached to you with ten thousand lines of barbed razor wire
Tethering you to grotesque images
Ghouls and demons and decaying corpses
And every time you turn your head away
The razor wire cuts a little deeper
Into your already tortured skin
Causing ever more persistent pain
And the images turn bleaker and blacker
The dust clouds from the building's bomb blast
Converging with the purple-black pre-tornado sky
The body parts strewn across the road
Blood and destruction everywhere
Yours intermingling with the death throes around you.

And your life hangs in the balance
Between a coma to shut out the pain
And an attempt to mitigate your response
To the battlefield your brain has created
In a mostly hopeless endeavor
To exorcise the terror, the fear
That paces your days
And invades your nights
Enveloping you like the razor wire
So enmeshed in it that the beginning strand
Is virtually impossible to find
As it is buried deep within you
Anchored with no slack to aid in removal.

And you scream in pain, in fear, in terror
And curse the perpetrators who put you there
Who took the razor wire in their professional, work-gloved hands
And slowly, each day, added another arc
Embedding the sharp, destructive razor points to your body
Slowly, year by year, twirling it in ever-tightening circles

Never listening to your pleas to stop
Just winding and winding
Until all that is visible is the cocoon of razor wire
The perpetrator's only concern
Is the durability of the razor wire
To maintain the entombment
That denies you life.

And you seemingly have no recourse
For the perpetrator has done an exemplary job
Followed the rule manual
With exactitude, allowing no exceptions
Concluding that the responsibility
For encasing you in razor wire
Was entirely your own
Because you refused to cooperate
With the pernicious attempts to vanquish your humanity
Your foolish, foolish proclamation
That you are human
Vaporized, extinguished by your perpetrator
Unperturbed by your razor wire-encapsulated existence.

And yet, the expectation is that you ignore your entrapment
That you function rationally
Even if your world is irrational
That you ignore your razor wire shroud
'Tis only a figment of your over-active imagination
As the perpetrator is a well-respected member of society
And when you scream from the pain
As the razor wire slashes you anew
You are deemed incoherent, a bastion of unfounded recollection
Instead of a person wrapped in a trauma shroud
And they tell you, it wasn't so bad, forgive and forget
Without understanding the extent of your trauma
Because you have no words for accurate description.

And you wish your perpetrators the same razor-wire cocoon
Condemning them to understanding your pain
In the only way possible
Because words are entirely inadequate
To convey the extent of the devastation inflicted on you
That extends year after year
With no respite, no rescue visible in the foreseeable future
No help,
Only rules designed to eviscerate any semblance of humanity
You install tortuous dehumanization into that razor-wire cocoon
Acting without remorse, without guilt, seeking only vindication
As you envision the massive deconstruction
Of your perpetrator's soul
Seeking not the perpetrator's death,
Only endless, excruciating terror
And so you pass your limited existence
In your entangled razor-wire cocoon.

Retribution

As the clock tolls out the midnight hour
Twelve strokes to relive your day
Trying to comprehend the incomprehensible
Trying to find some sort of order
Some sort of explanation
To at the very least
Compartmentalize the competing terrors
Into defined categories
Instead of a towering
Inescapable conglomeration
Of terrors, anger, fear
And a raging passion for retribution.

A retribution of scorched earth
Of inflicted pain
To match the pain contained
In your body, in your heart
In your soul
Realizing that you need
To temper this aspect of retribution
Because you don't want to kill
Your perpetrator, your abuser
You want to create hopelessness
Mixed with the pain
You want them to feel

The heaviness of being completely alone
Abandoned by every living creature
Entirely alone, unable to cry out for help
Because there is no one to hear
Those shrieks, those cries for mercy
Shrouded in silence

As they rise up into oblivion
And you watch them scream
Trying to initiate some kind,
Any kind of connection
But nobody is there because nobody cares.

You watch as they slowly realize
The world they now inhabit is ruled by fear
Ruled by unpredictability
Ruled by ever increasing confrontations
With those euphemistically called
Poor outcomes
And you watch as they try to escape
Knowing it is a useless endeavor
That they gradually accept
Because the fear has invaded
Their essence and removed their humanity
Shackling them to this storm of retribution.

And still the retribution you seek
Seems mild compared
To the hellscape they created
To destroy you
To annihilate you
Because you represented
A challenge to their power
To their omnipotence
A challenge not to be tolerated
By the powers that be
An indictment of their service to the almighty dollar

And the clock chimes out
The eleventh hour
Creating a desperation
A blinding need
To inflict a retribution so massive
So intolerable, so equivalent
To the lifetime horror experienced by you
To expose their Christian charity
As a pact with the devil
To torture as you have been tortured
Wishing they could live
In your nightmares.

And the clock strikes its last chime
Your contemplation of the horrors
Of the preceding day completed
Knowing that your dreams
Of retribution are just dreams
Offering a momentary escape
From the previous years of maltreatment
As you bestow on them
What they inflicted on you
Knowing that the next time
The clock begins its midnight countdown
You can begin another contemplation on retribution

Resilience

From Merriam-Webster: resilience is an ability to recover from or adjust easily to misfortune or change.

Well, you now understand why the word resilience
Generates such a negative response
Because it has nothing in common
With ongoing trauma
You're supposed to bounce back
To your pre-existing state
But how do you return to being a fetus?
Resilience assumes there was a before
And then an after
That there is a good thing to return to
That you emerge stronger
That there are no negative consequences
From a simple misfortune or trauma

Ah, but you know differently
Because it wasn't a simple trauma
The trauma encapsulated your life
It altered your perceptions
It was never-ending
Always maliciously conniving
To keep you in a cage of fear
Consumed by night terrors
And daytime scourges of debilitating memories
There is no prior time
Of goodness and light to return to
Because you can't remember a beginning
Only the everlasting dungeon of fear

From the APA: strategies to increase your capacity for resilience. 1. Build your connections 2. Foster wellness 3. Find purpose by being proactive 4. Embrace healthy thoughts.

Oh, how can there be
Such a limited understanding
Of life encased in ongoing trauma
That requires more than triage
How can you build connections
When you've been taught
That people are untrustworthy
That connections produce overwhelming fear
How do you foster wellness
When you live with disrupted sleep
And anxiety that rules your waking hours
When your purpose is simply
To find a way to maintain a connection to humanity

And thus, you are deemed a failure at resilience
Because you cannot manage any
Of the supposedly healthy ways
Of bouncing back from trauma
But maybe it isn't you who is a failure
Maybe it is the conception of resilience
Perhaps, just perhaps, resilience isn't the correct idea
For overcoming ongoing trauma
Because you are not resilient
The facile methodology can't
Teach you the strategies
That return you to the normal world
You are, instead, a survivor

From Oxford Learners Dictionary: a survivor is a person who continues to live, especially despite being nearly killed or experiencing great danger or difficulty

You live with great danger
As you attempt to live in a world
Where fear abounds in
Every breath you take,
Every action, every thought
And yet you still exist
Dreaming of ways to counteract
Or lessen the fear
Of minute possibilities of something
Untainted, even if it is merely
Uninterrupted sleep
You cling to your mantra
I am a survivor, I will survive even this.

Terror's Secret

The terror carefully guards a secret
Buried deep and guarded with toxic fumes
A secret so dangerous to the terror's existence
That it's coated with fear
And is kept in perpetual darkness
Wrapped in destructive waves of screaming
A banshee keening in high C
Endless, perpetual, irrational projections
Of terror, of fear, of abandonment
Telling you that you must succumb
To the power of the terror

Most people outside your trauma shroud
Don't know the terror's secret
Telling you to deal with the terror directly
To acknowledge your feelings
To work from the outside in
Such a dangerous, impossible, destructive solution
Because they don't understand
How the terror has corrupted your feelings
There is no happy or content or joy
They have all been reduced to
Dangerous, fear, trapped, abandoned
Triggers that cannot permeate the shroud from the outside

If you are very lucky, though
You can discover the terror's secret
Because you have struggled against its power
And somewhere deep inside
You have protected the essence of who you are
And discovered the terror's damning secret
That the terror LIES
And you can work through your trauma shroud
From the inside out
Knowing the terror will battle against you
By releasing a maelstrom of negative, cascading feelings
Trying to provoke you into believing its lie

But you have awakened your awareness
That you are a survivor
That even though the terror
Tries to manifest
What it considers its omnipotent power
You have within you
The power to slowly dismantle
That torturous trauma shroud
Not with feelings, they might come later
But with the knowledge
That you have the power of survivorship
An unbroken tie to the rest of humanity

The Return

You never really escape terror's mechanizations
It's insidious lurking, waiting
Waiting for the unexpected opening
To flood your body with
A tsunami of past pain
Because you weren't expecting
A betrayal of implicit trust
An attack on the self
You had worked so hard to create
You had torn a hole
In your trauma shroud
Struggled to leave the tornado
Of fear, of solitary confinement
Of the malignant, oppressive fealty
To the overwhelming power of terror
As it uses the threads of your trauma shroud
The ones still embedded
Deep in your psyche
Buried but not forgotten
To reel you back into
It's feral desire
To demolish the you
That you created
When you tore a rend
In your trauma shroud
Bringing you closer
To the hellfire of disingenuous existence
Existing, but not alive
Because the terror consumes you
But does not kill you
Because it needs pieces of you
To manifest its power
To manipulate your terror responses

Without you, the terror
Dissipates into foggy, ethereal nothingness
But you are a survivor
And next time, you won't be so unprepared
When trust is broken
You'll look for those embedded threads
And ready your defenses
Deciding if you need a machete
To slice away terror's connections
Knowing that it won't be the last time
That terror tries to ensnare you
Dragging you back to its cauldron of torment
But next time, you will also be stronger
Which will be necessary
Because the remaining deeply embedded threads
Are constructed out of razor wire
And you'll need more than a machete
But you have time to develop defenses
Against betrayed trust
Because you are a survivor.

Smog

Your life was embalmed
With the putrid smog
Of terror
The poisonous chemicals
Invading your lungs
Closing off your vision
Leaving the taste
Of ashen shame
In your mouth
Your body contorted
Doubled over
Seeking a wisp
A momentary reclamation
Of a breath
Instead of a gasp

And the smog has colored
Your view
Of yourself
Your interactions
Your entire world
Until the only thing you know
Is the deadening smog of terror
And your choice
Is to let it murder you
Or to learn to let it be
To ignore the rancid totality
It seeks to overwhelm you with
Enclosing yourself
In the world you created
Full of wonder and color
Creating an impenetrable shell
That promises safety
Locking out the voices
Proclaiming you are nothing

But sometimes
A raging wind
Blows away the smog
And you hear the other voices
That you matter
That you positively impacted
Other people's lives
And you are confused
And uncertain
Because the smog
Dictated your life for so long
That the other voices
Seem unreal, not false
But not connected
To your smog-encased reality

And you want to damn the smog
To create this new reality
But you know the smog
Still lives in swirling eddies
Just on the edge
Of the raging wind
And if the wind
Turns into a gentle breeze
Or dies to a nothingness
Of calm
And the smog will
Come hurtling back
Destroying everything in its path
And you will no longer have
Your impenetrable shell
Because the raging wind
Like a massive tornado

Shattered it
Tossing the pieces
Into oblivion

Oh, the risks are high
And the certainty of life
Outside of the smog
Is unknowable
Because you have no experience
Living there
And you scream in frustration
Knowing living in the smog
While familiar
Is also deadly
Perhaps not tomorrow
But sooner rather than later
And knowing living in the landscape
Devoid of the smog
Presents the unexperienced
For which you have
No predetermined patterns of action
Or understanding

And yet, there is a sense
A possibility
Of a great new exploration
But you look at it
With trepidation
Wondering
Are you strong enough
To remake your world
Without the knowledge
Or a template
Of how it should be

Knowing that failure is not an option
Because returning to the
Smog embalmed life
Will be returning to a coffin
Of nothingness.

Yes, the risks are high
But, in reality,
There is only one possibility
To choose life
For the smog will certainly destroy you
While the unknowable life
Outside of the smog
Will be a fearsome quest
With no predetermined outcome
No guaranteed treasure
Just a place in the world
A connection to other people
Good, bad, or indifferent
Scary and nerve-wracking
With screaming and tears
But living, not just existing
And possibilities
And the chance to breathe.

About the Author

Katrina N. Jirik graduated with a Ph.D. from the University of Minnesota. This book is her first published poetry work.

www.ingramcontent.com/pod-product-compliance
Lightning Source LLC
Chambersburg PA
CBHW072050160426
43197CB00014B/2704